THE GREAT OUTDOORS! →

Fishing

MC

Mason Crest

THE GREAT OUTDOORS!

THE GREAT OUTDOORS!

Fishing

JOHN PERRITANO

Mason Crest
450 Parkway Drive, Suite D
Broomall, PA 19008
www.masoncrest.com

© 2017 by Mason Crest, an imprint of National Highlights, Inc.

Printed and bound in the United States of America.

Series ISBN: 978-1-4222-3565-2
Hardback ISBN: 978-1-4222-3568-3
EBook ISBN: 978-1-4222-8313-4

First printing
1 3 5 7 9 8 6 4 2

Produced by Shoreline Publishing Group LLC
Santa Barbara, California
Editorial Director: James Buckley Jr.
Designer: Patty Kelley
Production: Sandy Gordon
www.shorelinepublishing.com

Cover photographs by Piotr Wawrzyniuk/Dreamstime.com.

Library of Congress Cataloging-in-Publication Data is on file with the publisher.

CONTENTS

KEY ICONS TO LOOK FOR

Words to Understand: These words with their easy-to-understand definitions will increase the reader's understanding of the text, while building vocabulary skills.

Sidebars: This boxed material within the main text allows readers to build knowledge, gain insights, explore possibilities, and broaden their perspectives by weaving together additional information to provide realistic and holistic perspectives.

Research Projects: Readers are pointed toward areas of further inquiry connected to each chapter. Suggestions are provided for projects that encourage deeper research and analysis.

Text-Dependent Questions: These questions send the reader back to the text for more careful attention to the evidence presented here.

Series Glossary of Key Terms: This back-of-the-book glossary contains terminology used throughout this series. Words found here increase the reader's ability to read and comprehend higher-level books and articles in this field.

Educational Videos: Readers can view videos by scanning our QR codes, providing them with additional educational content to supplement the text. Examples include news coverage, moments in history, speeches, iconic sports moments and much more!

Fish On!

he brook trout sat behind the rock as the rushing water of a Connecticut river flowed wildly past its torpedo-shaped body. The fisherman, wearing a khaki fishing vest, hat, and waders faced the creature head-on.

He stood in the river on a slippery underwater rock. Grasping a fly rod firmly with his right hand, the angler tried to entice the fish to bite a fuzzy artificial bait tied to the end of the line. This particular lure was a series of threads and knots bound together to look like a small brown moth.

One cast . . . two casts . . . three and then four. Most were perfect. The feathery "fly" hit the water with a soft splash and performed an aquatic two-step as it danced in front of the trout. The fly jigged. It shimmied. It jerked. The fish ignored it. The fisherman made cast after frustrating cast. The fish did not bite.

You might hear a fisherman referred to as an angler. The name comes from the hooks fishermen use. Fishing hooks are curved, or angled. However, if you fish with just a net, you're just a fisherman.

The idea in fly fishing is to make the fish believe the fly is real. The fisherman was failing miserably in this attempt. The stubborn fish stayed near the rock, refusing to pay attention. The trout sometimes jumped into the air scooping up a mouthful of real bugs. Most of the time, however, the creature just drifted.

The sun finally began to set. The wind picked up, sending a chill down the river. The fisherman was hungry. He called it quits, happy that even though he hadn't caught a fish, it was a day well spent.

 WHAT'S THAT WORD?

Fishing has a language all its own. Different methods have different terms. Here are a few general terms every fisherman should know and that will come up later in this book.

- **Bait:** the lure, artificial or natural, that attracts fish
- **Baitfish:** small fish that larger fish like to eat
- **Barb:** the sharp point on the fish hook that holds the fish
- **Catch and Release:** catching a fish and releasing it back into the water
- **Chum:** fish bones, guts and bloods used as bait
- **Reel:** device that holds the fishing line
- **Sinker:** a weight that allows the fishing line to sink
- **Tackle box:** the box that holds lures, line, hooks, and other fishing necessities

They never saw each other again, the brook trout and fisherman. As he slunk away, the fishing writer Izaak Walton came to mind: "As no man is born an artist, so no man is born an angler."

Fish On!

Whether you use fly or reel, worm or cricket, fishing is more than a sport—it is a way of life and one of the most popular pastimes around. Yet, not everyone fishes the same way. Some people fish from a boat, others from the banks of a lake. A brave few fish in canoes or kayaks.

On a river or at a lake, fishing is a great way to spend time with family.

Some, like the fisherman above, use up an enormous amount of energy and time making cast after cast. Others sit on a dock, drop a line in the water, and take a nap or read a book. Some fishing methods are adventurous. A few are even dangerous.

Short History of Fishing

People have been fishing for centuries. They fished first for food using sharpened branches to spear their prey. They then carved hooks made from wood, bone, and stone. The hooks were shaved to a sharp point and tied to lines of woven plant fibers.

The ancient Egyptians fished the Nile River using rods and nets. The ancient Chinese used cooked rice as bait.

This painting shows an ancient Egyptian using a net to haul in fish.

Fly fishing gear includes reels, flies, a landing net, and a basket for fish.

As the centuries passed, the tools of fishing, especially rods, lines, and hooks evolved. People fished less for food and more for sport. The earliest written work devoted to recreational fishing was published in 1496. Yet, it wasn't until Englishman Izaak Walton wrote *The Complete Angler* in 1653 that sport fishing really took off.

Today, fishing has gone way beyond sharpened sticks and bone hooks. Rods are so light, it is as if you're casting with a feather. You can buy lures with cameras, and an underwater sonar device that can track fish in any direction as they swim.

Turn the page and drop your bait. See if you can catch a big one!

CHAPTER 1

Freshwater Fishing

 he river where that Connecticut fisherman spent hours casting was a freshwater fishery, one of the prime trout fishing areas in New England. Such freshwater fisheries are the most popular places to fish. Freshwater contains little or no salt. About 40 percent of all fish live in freshwater **ecosystems**, including trout, walleye, salmon, and catfish, among others.

 WORDS TO UNDERSTAND

ecosystems an environment shared by many organisms

eddies smalls whirls of flowing water

lethargic having low energy, very tired

predators animals that eat other animals to survive

troll fish by dragging a baited line from the back of a boat

Fishing rods are designed to bend very far without breaking.

Freshwater fishing takes place not only on rivers, but in streams, lakes, reservoirs, and ponds. People fish these areas from shore, boat, the top of a bridge, or dock. Each location presents its own challenges, and each fish behaves differently, depending on their habitat.

Freshwater offers plenty of places for fish to hide and feed. Docks, logs, rocks, and shaded areas protect fish from natural **predators**— including humans.

Different Habitats

Not all freshwater fishing is created equal. Fishing rivers and streams is much different from fishing ponds and lakes. For one thing, rivers and streams are always on the move. Fish behave differently when water is moving. They often hide along river banks where rushing water has created an undercut. Fish will slink behind overhanging trees, stay near bushes, or retreat to eddies where water swirls around rocks and logs.

When a river or stream curves, the rushing water carries food for the fish to eat. The water slows as it bumps up against rocks or fallen trees. When that happens, the water splits, creating a "pocket" for fish to hide. Not only do these areas provide shelter, but it is also an aquatic supermarket where the rushing river deposits food (dead bugs, insect larvae, fish eggs, and other treats).

Unlike lakes and ponds, rivers often have areas under the water where the riverbed drops off. As the water passes over these geologic formations, it slows and sinks, depositing food in deep water away from the rushing current.

Water near a dam or waterfall is also a good place to look for fish. The rushing water carves a hole in the stream bottom where fish will meet to feed. Some fish, such as salmon, swim upstream but dams and waterfalls block their journey. Salmon fishermen understandably love these areas.

Changing Seasons

Fish also behave differently depending on the seasons, as anyone who has fished Lake George in upstate New York can tell you. Lake George is a jewel of a lake. The water is so clean that people drink directly from it. Lake George is also brimming with many fish species, including perch, lake trout, largemouth bass, smallmouth bass, and others.

Regardless of whether a person has been fishing for years or is just starting out, the basics of fishing are still the same. Each fisherman has to:

prepare their reel and line. The reel holds the line. The line is threaded through the eyelets of the rod.

Reel attached to rod

Tying a hook to line

attach a hook. Hooks come in all shapes and sizes and are knotted to the end of the line. Picking the right hook is essential. The bigger the fish, the bigger the hook. Know what you're fishing for and be smart about your hooks. When you get a nibble a fisherman has to "set" the hook to make sure it's firmly planted in the fish's mouth.

attach the bait. This is where fishing gets complicated. Some fishermen use live bait, such as worms and minnows (small fish). Other fishermen use artificial bait, or lures. Lures look, sound and even smell like live bait. Picking the right bait, real or not, is complicated. Different fish are attracted to different types of bait.

Worms: classic bait

Casting for fish

cast and retrieve. Casting is an art. Fly fishermen, for example, use many techniques to put make their bait look as natural as possible. Once the fly is on the water, a fishermen will "strip" or pull in the line hoping to attract a fish. Bass fishermen will often bait their hooks with minnows and **troll** for fish by motoring slowly down the lake. Take care in reeling the fish in. You don't want to lose it.

In the spring, fishing is great. The water is cool, and the fish hang near the surface hoping to catch their breakfast, lunch, and dinner. By August, however, the environment of the lake changes drastically. The summer sun has turned lake water into a tepid pool. The fish become **lethargic**. They expend little energy and hang out in deep areas to cool off. They seldom rise to the surface to feed.

All that changes as summer turns to fall. The water and air temperature cool the lake, energizing the fish that are back near the surface, hungry as ever.

 ## TEXT DEPENDENT QUESTIONS

1. Name three types of freshwater fisheries.

2. How many species of fish live in freshwater?

3. Where is Lake George?

 ## RESEARCH PROJECT

Research and create a list of the best places to fish in your community or the surrounding area. Are these places mostly freshwater fisheries, or saltwater habitats? What types of fish can you find in each of the spots?

Getting Started:
Tips on How to Fish

CHAPTER 2

Fishing Methods

person can fish any way they choose. Along with rods and reels, fishermen use spears, nets, and even bows and arrows (more on that later). Yet, the two most basic methods are fly fishing and spin casting. Although each uses different gear, both can be done on lakes, streams, ponds, rivers and in oceans.

 WORDS TO UNDERSTAND

aquatic relating to water

auger a hand tool with a sharp, corkscrew-like blade that cuts a hole in the ice

entice attract

invasive species a type of animal not native to a habitat whose introduction causes problems for the habitat

nymphs juvenile forms of insects

To a fish, these fuzzy flies look like real food . . . until it's too late!

Fly fishing is as the name suggests—fishing with flies, although the bugs one uses are not real. For many, fly fishing is an art as well as a science. The purpose is to entice a fish by using an artificial lure that looks and acts like a real bug. Some fishermen will tie their own flies by hand. Some flies are made to sink in the water. They are called "wet" flies. Other flies float on the surface. They are called "dry" flies.

Matching the Hatch

For many, dry fly fishing is the most exciting. The fly sits on top of the water trying to **entice** the fish to come to the surface. Figuring out what the fish are eating is difficult. Fish are fussy eaters, so selecting the right fly is essential.

Successful fly fishers will try to "match the hatch." In other words, they try to select flies that look like those that are on the water at that precise moment. These can include **nymphs** (insects that just hatch but don't fly) and adults (insects that can fly).

Matching the hatch is very complicated. Before a fisherman begins casting, he or she will look at the water to see what type of insects are floating on the surface or hovering above. The fisherman will then pluck a fly from the surface of the water and take a good look at it. Some of the insects they find can be drifting nymphs, emerging adults, or insects that have just laid their eggs. The fisherman then looks into his or her fly box to pick out a fly that resembles those on the water.

Some flies are tied to look like other insects, including grasshoppers and ants. Some are colorful and have rubber legs dangling from them.

An attracter is a variety of fly not tied to look like any specific insect. They are often colorful. Streamers are tied to look like a baitfish or some other large **aquatic** prey. Some are tied to look like minnows and caterpillars. Some flies are tied to look like non-aquatic critters, such as worms.

Cast Off

lthough you might have the right type of fly on the end of your line, you won't catch a fish until you cast. This is where science plays an important role.

Fly fishing line is heavy enough to send the fly to its destination on its own. During a cast, the fly line trails behind the rod tip. Energy created during the back cast is transferred through the line during the front cast, carrying the fly forward.

 FINICKY FISH

Many species of fish are opportunistic eaters. In other words, if they see an insect that looks close enough to one they have eaten before, they will eat it again. Many fish species, such as trout, especially like to dine on nymphs. Nymphs spend most of their time living under the surface of the water. They will also hang out along river and streambeds. They are an abundant source of food.

Hold the rod with one hand and turn the handle on the spin reel with the other.

There are many different ways to cast a fly. A roll cast can be used to fish a narrow stream flanked by overhanging trees. A sidearm cast works well if it is windy, or if you want to place the fly in the water under tree branches.

Spin-Casting

S pin-casting is a much easier way to fish. Spin-casting uses the weight of metal lures (not the line) to move the fishing line forward. The line is wound around a spool on the reel that doesn't move. As the forward cast is made, the line peels off the spool with little resistance. As such, the line rarely is snarled.

Most spin casting reels are open-faced. On these reels is a "bail" that holds the line in place. After a cast, all a fisherman has to do is turn the hand crank, which forces the bail to snap back into place, allowing the line to become stationary.

Some spin cast reels require the fisherman to grasp the line to control the cast. Other models have a release mechanism, such as push button for line control.

Ice Fishing

Just because it is snowing and freezing outside doesn't mean a person can't fish. In many northern climes, such as New England, northern New York, Wisconsin, and Minnesota, fishing on a frozen lake, also called ice fishing, is a religion.

Some ice fishermen have taken great pains to make sure they are comfortable when they are out on the ice. They have elaborate cabins (some with TVs, heaters, and microwave ovens) to fish from. Others, however, fish more primitively. They sit out on the ice on a portable chair or on a milk crate, dangling a line into a hole cut out of the frozen surface.

Staying warm and being patient are the ice fisherman's biggest needs.

Still others spend their day angling away in simple huts called shanties, which can be built out of plywood, scraps of lumber or discarded steel. Some have skids on the bottom so they can be hooked up to the back of a pickup truck and towed out on the ice.

Unlike other types of fishing, ice fishing does not require a rod or reel, although you can certainly use one. The first thing an ice fisherman has to do is cut a hole in the ice using an auger.

Once the hole is made, the fisherman can drop a line down and wait for the fish to bite. Most ice fishermen use tip-ups that they bait. Tip-ups have a line and a hook. Tip-ups also allow ice fishermen to bait several holes at once. When a fish takes the bait, a marker or a flag "tips up." That's when the fisherman knows there's a fish on the line.

The waiting pays off when you land a tasty (very chilly) fish.

Human 1, Catfish 0. Brave noodlers take on large fish with their bare hands.

Extreme Fishing

Have you ever heard of "noodling?" It has nothing to do with pasta. However, it does have everything to do with catching catfish with your bare hands. Catfish spend most of their time near rocks and logs. They rarely swim to the top. Catfish are big, too. They can tip the scales at 75 pounds (34 kg).

A noodler is a person who catches catfish with their hands. They wade along the riverbank and stick their arms under the water. They then feel around for a catfish. When a noodler hits pay dirt, they'll put their hands down the fish's mouth and haul it to the top.

Some noodlers wear tight-fitting leather gloves to guard their hands and arms. Others use flat-bottom boats to look for a catfish nest. When they find one, they'll toss bags of rock overboard so the fish cannot escape. Hand in, fish out. You get the idea.

Other people like to catch fish using bows and arrows. It's called aerial bow-fishing. As the name suggests, aerial bow-fishing combines archery and fishing. Riding in fast-moving boats, bow fishers speedily motor down lakes and rivers aiming their weapons at the fish that jump out of the water.

One of the most popular jumping fish is the Asian silver carp, an **invasive species** that can weigh up to 100 pounds (45.3 kg).

In aerial bow-fishing, the fisherman stands near the rear or side of the boat. They take aim when the fish rocket out of the water. The arrow is tied to a reel mounted on the side of the bow. When the arrow flies and hits its mark, the line tightens. The captain stops the boat so the fish can be pulled in.

It's a wild way to fish. A missed shot is a missed opportunity. You have to reel in your arrow quickly for another shot. The key is to watch for a fish that jumps unusually high and hangs in the air, just as Michael Jordan, the great basketball player, used to do. If you miss, a handbrake mounted on the bow will stop the arrow so it doesn't fly all the way out.

Some fishermen fish as they swim. It's called skishing. The idea is to hook a big fish while swimming in the ocean. Once the beast is hooked, the fish will tow the skisherman through the water. Like all extreme fishing methods, there are hazards to skishing, including rip tides, currents and getting struck by a passing boat.

 ## TEXT DEPENDENT QUESTIONS

1. What is a nymph?

2. What does it mean to "match the hatch?"

3. How do "noodlers" fish?

 ## RESEARCH PROJECT

Interview a fisherman in your local community. Find out what he or she fishes for and what methods and bait they use.

Different Ways to
Go Fishing

CHAPTER 3

Get Great Gear

ishing can be a solitary pursuit. It can also be a great way to spend time with family and friends. But, when you get right down to it, the goal of fishing is to catch fish. Having the right gear goes a long way in fulfilling that quest.

In recent years, the centuries-old battle between human and fish has become lopsided because of the high-tech gear on the market. In the old days, a fisherman

 WORDS TO UNDERSTAND

biodegrade decay naturally over time

monofilament an untwisted single strand of artificial fiber

polarized treated to reduce some forms of sunlight

shank the long, narrow part of a hook

sutures material used for surgical stitching

The electronics in this SmartRod let the angler know more about a fish strike.

would have to keep an eye on the end of his or her line to see if a fish had taken the bait. Any jerk or tug was a cause for celebration.

A computerized rod called the SmartRod takes all the guess work out of telling if a fish is on the line. The SmartRod has an electronic accelerometer that alerts a fisherman when a fish touches the line. An accelerometer is a device that measures vibrations, and is often used in buildings, on airliners, and in spacecraft.

When a fish touches the line, a sound or light alarm goes off. Once the hook is set, the rod automatically shuts itself down as the fisherman starts reeling in the fish. It will then reset itself for the next cast.

A Long, Thin Line

When fishermen goes out on the water, they carry with them a spool of plastic **monofilament** fishing line. Yet, more and more fishermen are using braided line woven from materials used in bulletproof vests and surgical **sutures** that are as thin as dental floss.

Thinner lines are important when trying to hook a big fish, especially in salt water. Thinner, lighter lines mean an angler can catch a trophy-sized tuna or marlin while the boat is stationary, instead of trolling the bait behind a boat. On fresh water, the braided lines are so sensitive that when a big bass touches it, you can immediately set the hook.

Tackle Box

The tackle box is one of the most important pieces of equipment a fisherman can have. A well-stocked box, which can easily be transported from place to place, should contain extra hooks, additional line, sinkers, a nail clipper (easy to cut line with), a knife, and a small first aid kit (you never know when you will stick yourself with a hook.)

Fishermen are always changing lures, and the most experienced fishermen will kept them in small plastic cases in the box. Try not to mix your trout lures with your bass lures, however. It will save time when you reach for a new one.

Having an assortment of bobbers, or floaters, will help you know when a fish bites. Bobbers float on top of the water while the bait dangles from a line under the surface. When a fish hits the bait, the bobber sinks. That's your cue to set the hook and begin reeling the fish in.

Sinkers are also an important part of any well-stocked tackle box. A hook and worm do not weigh all that much. By tying a sinker or two to towards the end of the line, you will make sure that the bait is getting down below the surface where it should be. Sinkers come in all shapes and sizes. Some are split. They are called "split shot." The fishing line goes between the teeth

A tackle box carries almost all the gear that someone going fishing needs.

of the sinker, which you then squeeze together. Others sinkers are bell-shaped.

It is also important to have pliers in your tackle box. They come in handy when pulling hooks out.

What to Wear

nlike basketball players or football players, fishermen don't need to wear a uniform. Jeans and T-shirt always work best. However, there are certain types of fishing apparel that will make your fishing trip more rewarding. Of course, sunscreen is important anytime you are outdoors, too.

Waders (far right) are essential for rivers and streams. Waders are like raincoats for your legs. Some are thigh-high, others come up to your chest. Waders keep the water out as you walk across the river or streambed. If you're going to wear waders, you will need to put on a

VESTS AND FLOATING FLY BOXES

No fly fisher should be without a multi-pocket vest and a floating fly box. If you're fishing a stream or river, your tackle box is going to be on the shore. It's too big to carry to the middle of the stream—and why would you anyway?

Instead, slip on a fishing vest. It can carry all your essential tools and supplies, including additional line, lures, and sinkers. Also, keep your flies in a floating fly box. A floating box will keep your flies from going under if you accidentally drop them in the water.

special pair of boots. These boots are waterproof and will help prevent you from slipping if you misstep.

A hat is also important. Hats keep the sun off your head and face. It also keeps sunlight out of your eyes. Some hats have wide brims. Others come with a mosquito net. Trout fishermen often wear these hats to keep the bugs out of their face.

Many fishermen, whether on the ocean or on a river, will also wear **polarized** glasses to cut down on sun glare. These sunglasses can help you spot a fish as it tries to blend into its surroundings.

Hi-Def Cameras

For years, fishermen have used fish finders—mini-underwater sonar devices—to find where the fish were lurking. When the device found a school of fish, it beeped. You could then look on a tiny screen and see the images created by the finder.

These days, anglers have graduated to high-definition sonar devices that see every ridge and shelf below the water in a 360-degree sweep. The devices give anglers a much clearer indication of what a lake or river bottom looks like and more exact readout as to where the fish are hiding.

Fish on camera!

Feeling a fish strike at the end of the line and then swim away can be one of the most frustrating parts of fishing. Small underwater cameras now allow a fisherman to see the fish as they swim up to the bait. One model, Strike Cam, is placed between the main fishing line and lure. Its lens focuses on the lure, keeping a watchful eye on it along with the surrounding water.

The American Sportfishing Association says as many as 33 million people, aged 16 or older, go fishing, mostly on freshwater lakes and rivers. They spend about $48 million a year on equipment, licenses, and fishing gear. Anglers support more than 828,000 jobs in the United States, including bait stores, hotels, and other businesses. There are more fishermen in Florida (3 million) than in any other state.

By studying the video footage, a fisherman can better understand which lures work, and which do not.

Green Fishing

aise your hand if you have ever gone fishing and got your line tangled high on a tree branch or snagged on a submerged log. After several minutes of pulling, you did the only thing you could do—cut the line. Not only did you lose a good portion of the line, but you also lost an expensive lure.

While cutting the line has always been the logical thing to do, it was not environmentally friendly. Discarded fishing line doesn't disappear overnight. In fact it takes 600 years to biodegrade. Not only does the line take a long time to decay, it can also be an immediate hazard to boat propellers and wildlife, especially birds and fish.

Many fishermen are opting these days to fish green by using biodegradable line that takes five years to disappear. Moreover, lead sinkers that can last in the environment thousands of years are slowly being replaced by sinkers made out of tungsten and brass, which are more environmentally friendly.

To keep the green theme going, fishermen who practice catch-and-release (which means to let the fish go back to the water quickly after catching it) are starting to use barbless hooks, which reduce injury to the fish. Some barbless hooks are "circle" hooks, in which the point is turned back towards the **shank**. Circle hooks are designed to embed in the corner of a fish's mouth or jaw without injuring the fish.

TEXT DEPENDENT QUESTIONS

1. How does a SmartRod work?

2. How long does it take fishing line to decay in the environment?

3. Why do some fishermen use "barbless" hooks?

RESEARCH PROJECT

Create a computer slideshow showing how pollution is affecting the nation's saltwater and freshwater fishing habitats.

Get Your Gear! How to Choose the Right Fishing Tools for You

Fishing Adventures

he angler was at it again. This time he was not casting in a river nor looking for a trout. His field of dreams this day was the Long Island Sound off the Connecticut coast.

The old men at the bait and tackle shop bragged that their particular part of the sound brimmed with striped sea bass some, they said, as "big as this," stretching their arms beyond their shoulders. "Good eatin,'" they added, and fun to catch. The fisherman wanted in.

 WORDS TO UNDERSTAND

caddisflies moth-like insects often found in freshwater habitats

gaff a pole with a large hook on the end

mayflies aquatic insects known for their short lifespan

temperate mild

On a May day early in the misty morning, the fisherman set out to test his luck. He chartered a boat out of a New England cove and told the captain to take him where the fish were.

The captain happily obliged, motoring to a spot known as the "race," a 3.5-mile (5.6 km) wide current of water that serves as the main entrance to the sound. It is here the giant stripers feed, the captain said.

The boat's first mate baited a hook shaped like an umbrella, which could handle more than one fish. When the line hit the water, the boat trolled the sea lane for a bite.

The fisherman felt a tug about an hour into the cruise. It was faint at first, but a tug nonetheless. Then it happened again.

Bam! The third felt as if a hand had come up, grabbed the fishing pole, and bent the rod toward the sea.

"Fish on!" the mate yelled.

The captain maneuvered the boat to make the fight easier. The fishermen battled. He pulled up on the rod…over and over…eventually

Sport fishing boats roar out on to the ocean in search of large game fish.

Some fish are so heavy, anglers are strapped to a fighting chair!

more than six times. He reeled the line in slowly with each pull. The fish fought as if its life depended on it.

It did.

Finally, the fisherman had landed his catch: two stripers, one bluefish. Each had a firm grip on the umbrella hook. One striper was legal size, the other not. Back into the water it went.

The adventure had paid off. The old men at the bait store were right—stripers were tasty.

Thrill of the Catch

Whether you're fishing for stripers in Long Island Sound or bonefish in Belize, fishing for so-called "sport fish" can be exciting, not because of their value as food, but because they are thrilling to catch. Sport fish put up a good fight.

Tuna is among the most popular sport fish, testing a fisherman's stamina, patience, and strength. There are nearly 50 species and most live in tropical and temperate water.

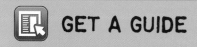
A good guide is worth his or her weight in chum. Guides are local fishing experts. They know where the fish are biting and what they are eating. They know what species everyone is pulling in, and which ones they are not.

Those who have never gone tuna fishing before would benefit by chartering a boat and getting help from an experienced crew. Knowing where tuna hang out is extremely important. Anglers will target Atlantic species from September to November. During that time, tuna follow warm water currents that linger about 5 miles offshore.

One of the best spots for tuna fishing is off Prince Edward Island and Nova Scotia in Canada, where yellowfins can top out at 350 pounds (159 kg) and bluefins can tip the scales at 1,000 pounds (454 kg). Sport fishermen will also travel to Australia from May to July for yellowfin and bluefin.

Fishing for such large species is not the same as fishing for brook trout. Tuna fishermen often use a chum slick to lure the fish to the boat. Chum is fish bait, a mixture of fish bones, heads, and blood, a tasty diet for tuna, sharks, and other sport fish.

When fishing for tuna, the tackle must be able to withstand the fight the 400 pound (181 kg) fish will put up. Fishermen will also use a **gaff** to stab and lift the fish into the boat.

While tuna fishing is a great adventure, nothing is as exciting as seeing a blue marlin, with its sword-like snout and huge sailfin, break the water's surface and rocket through the air.

For many anglers, marlin fishing is the high point of saltwater sport fishing. The fish's size and power make it an incredible fish to catch. Marlin can be found in the Atlantic and Pacific oceans following schools of small tuna and other baitfish.

The mighty marlin usually gives anglers a great fight.

Landing an Alaskan salmon with help from a guide's net.

The waters off the U.S. Virgin Islands are one of the prime marlin fishing grounds, especially off the eastern end of St. Thomas. The fish in this area weigh on average 300 pounds (136 kg), although it's not uncommon to spot a 500-pounder (226 kg).

Costa Rica, a country in Central America, is another hot-spot for marlin-fishing. Marlin feed close to the shore during Costa Rica's dry season, which lasts from December through March.

Salmon Adventures

In Alaska, on the Kenai River, anglers will stand shoulder-to-shoulder hoping to land one of the most popular sport fish in the world—the king, or Chinook salmon. The Kenai River, located on the Kenai Peninsula, is the most heavily-fished river in the state. It is common to catch a 50-pound (23 kg) king on the Kenai.

During the spring, king salmon make their way from the Pacific Ocean to the Kenai and other Alaskan rivers to spawn. Adult females deposit their eggs on gravel beds, where they wait to be fertilized by the male.

Chinook can spend from one year to eight years in the Pacific before returning inland. Most come back after three or four years at sea.

Alaska King
Salmon Adventures

The Kenai River turns red each spring (the color of the Chinook) as the fish make their way upstream, which makes the river a prime fishing ground. Chinook, which range in size from 25 to 126 pounds (11 to 71 kg), are a tasty fish, which makes it a prized catch. Anglers from all over the world come to Alaska and hire guides to take them to the best fishing areas.

Others will go on their own, standing on the overcrowded river bank, their lines baited with a variety of enticements including salmon eggs.

Trout Adventures

"A trout is a moment of beauty known only to those who seek it," Arnold Gingrich, a writer and fisherman once wrote. Some 11 million anglers in the United States and Canada know exactly what Gingrich was talking about.

The Catskills are one of many places in the Northeast with great fishing.

MAJOR LEAGUE FISHING

While Izaak Walton and Arnold Gingrich might have liked the solitary pursuit of angling, other fishermen are more competitive, especially bass fishermen. They face each other in tournaments.

Becoming a pro bass fisherman is not for everyone. For one thing it is not cheap. In fact, the best bass pro fishermen had to work other jobs while they pursued their dreams. Hundreds of factors come into play at tournaments. And like every other sport, bass fishermen have to practice.

Pro bass fisherman Skeet Rees shows off his winning catch.

North America has some of the best trout fishing in the world, and most of it is open to the public and easy to access. In New York state, in the heart of the Catskill Mountains, sits a river called the Beaverkill, where Gingrich use to fish. The river flows almost 44 miles (71 km) through the mountains before it meets up with the East Branch of the Delaware River.

The Beaverkill is home to a variety of insects. **Caddisflies** and **mayflies** are so thick at times that an angler will sometimes wonder if they are standing in the middle of a snow storm. The best time to fish is right when trout seasons opens each April. For 10 weeks, the flies will hatch and the trout will bite.

In the West, Montana has a well-earned reputation as perhaps the best trout fishery in North America, while in New England the Battenkill River, a nearly 60-mile (97 km) waterway that runs from Vermont into New York, is also a trout fisherman's paradise.

Whether you fish in a pond, a stream, a river, or on the mighty ocean, if you're fishing . . . you're in paradise!

 TEXT DEPENDENT QUESTIONS

1. How many species of tuna are there?

2. In which state is the Kenai River located?

3. What is the job of a fishing guide?

 RESEARCH PROJECT

Everyone has a fish story. What's yours? Write a two page report on a fishing trip you might have taken. If you have never been fishing, write a short story about what the perfect fishing trip might be.

FIND OUT MORE

WEBSITES

www.fieldandstream.com/articles/fishing/saltwater/2006/
12/25-tips-saltwater-fishing
One of the top outdoor magazines offers fishing tips.

www.freshwater-fishing.org/
Read stories of some about the greatest anglers of all time.

www.dec.ny.gov/outdoor/fishing.html
This is one of many state sites that provide information about sport fishing, licenses, seasons, and types of fish.

www.gutenberg.org/files/9198/9198-h/9198-h.htm
Read over the classic text of *The Complete Angler* by Izaak Walton in this ebook version.

BOOKS

Bourne, Wade. *Basic Fishing: A Beginner's Guide.* New York: Skyhorse Publishing, 2015.

Cermele, Joe: *The Total Fishing Manual (Field and Stream).* San Francisco: Weldon Owen, 2013.

Howard, Melanie. *Freshwater Fishing for Kids (Into the Great Outdoors).* Mankato, Minn.: Capstone Press, 2012.

Morey, Shaun. *Incredible—and True!—Fishing Stories.* New York: Workman Publishing, 2014.

bushcraft wilderness skills, named for the remote bush country of Australia

camouflage a pattern or disguise in clothing designed to make it blend into the surroundings

conservation the act of preserving or protecting, such as an environment or species

ecosystem the habitats of species and the ways that species interact with each other

friction the resistance that happens when two surfaces rub together

insulation protection from something, such as extreme hot or cold

layering adding layers of clothing to stay warm and removing layers to cool off.

rewilding returning to a more natural state

synthetic man-made, often to imitate a natural material

traction the grip or contact that an object has with another surface

wake the waves produced by the movement of a boat

INDEX

PHOTO CREDITS

(Dreamstime.com: DT; Dollarphotos.com: Dollar) KcMatt/DT 6; Andrei Katyshev/DT 8; Goldenkb/DT 9; Sandra Cunningham/DT 11; Goodluz/DT 12; Mikhail Dudarev/DT 13; Prochasson Frederic/DT 14t; Dobphoto/DT 14cl; Sergiy Palamarchuk/DT 14cr; Justinhoffma-noutdoors/DT 14b; Tommy Hammarsten/DT 18; Bert Folsom/DT 20; oleshkonti/Dollar 22; Stephen McSweeny/DT 23; Ron Chapple/DT 24; David Ryznar/DT 25; Jason Lindsay/Alamy 26; biker3/Dollar 28; Courtesy SmartRod 30; Arenacreative/DT 31; Bert Folsom/DT 32; Lju-pco Smokovski/DT 33; Courtesy AquaVu 33; Sebastian Czapnik/DT 36; Steven Rivieccio/DT 38; Southerncoastcharters.com.au 39; Dmitry Chulov/DT 40; Lunamarina/DT 41; Lawrence Weslowski Jr./DT 42; Peter Zachar/DT 43; Terry Schmitt/UPI/Newscom 44.

ABOUT THE AUTHOR

Whether it is fishing for trout in New England, salmon in Alaska, or bonefish in Belize, author **John Perritano** always has his fly rod (and his spin caster) in the back of his truck. Perritano has written numerous articles and books (many on fishing). He lives in Southbury, Connecticut, about a quarter-mile away from a trout stream.